Asperger's (ASD) Autism Spectrum Disorder

–

A Workplace Guide

Written and published

by

Rosita Bird

Abstract: This booklet aims to provide enough information to foster a better understanding and acceptance in the workplace among both employers and employees of the condition of Asperger's Syndrome, (ASD) which is one of the three recognized types of Autism. It provides an introduction to the signs and symptoms and how best to interact, communicate and cope with any issues that may occur.

Keywords: Autism—Asperger's, Employers and employees guide providing information and coping strategies for working with Asperger's.

Index

Asperger's – A Workplace Guide

Introduction – What is Autism?

Autism was a term first used by a psychiatrist called Eugen Bleuler in 1908. At that time, he used it to describe a schizophrenic patient who had withdrawn into his own world. The word autós is a Greek word which meant self, and the word autism was used by Bleuler to mean morbid self-admiration and withdrawal within self. There are still arguments over whether it has something to do with overindulgence, labelled by some as spoilt brat syndrome. There are still those who debate how much of these traits can be traced to upbringing. The first pioneers who did research into autism were Hans Asperger and Leo Kanner. This is where the name Asperger's comes from and describes those children who were very able, while Kanner described children with more severe symptoms. They were working separately in the 1940s. Their views remained useful for physicians for the next three decades.

It is important to understand that autism is a developmental disability from birth that is caused by neurological differences in the brain and is not an illness or disease that requires curing. It is known that there are many more men on the spectrum than women. The easiest way to describe this is being wired up differently. Autism has an effect on how people perceive the world and how they interact with others. Those with (ASD) Autistic Spectrum Disorder are people who see, hear, and feel the world differently from other people. All autistic people share certain difficulties, but being autistic will affect them in different ways. Some autistic people will have learning disabilities, mental health issues, or other more complex conditions associated with autism such as misophonia, savant, obsessive compulsive disorder (OCD) mysophobia, depression, tourette syndrome and epilepsy. These different conditions all require different kinds of support. This does not mean any one person will have all of these conditions.

While it is statistically accepted that there are more men than women who have autism, it does not mean that there are not actually as many women who have autism. The reason most recently accepted is that women are better at masking their traits. Today, an increasing number of women are being diagnosed for this condition. With the right kind of support it is possible that people on the autistic spectrum can learn and develop and therefore be helped to live a more productive life. With the right kind of support it is possible that people on the autistic spectrum can learn and develop and therefore be helped to live a more fulfilling life of their own choosing. ASD has a wide umbrella, and while the most severe may need a lot of help and support to enable them to live independently, there are others who are quite able to support and look after themselves, including being able to work independently and successfully. The various conditions that may be associated with autism are as follows:-

Misophonia

Misophonia is a deep sensitivity to certain noises. The sound most of us hate is fingernails dragged on a blackboard, which makes our hair stand on end; this is one most of us can sympathize with. Most of us can block out and cope with the sounds around us but for some people they will be the focus of their attention and therefore dominate their thoughts. This can irritate and cause distress. It is impossible to list all the sounds that might cause this problem but here is a list of a few:- eating sounds like chewing (this is quite a common one as many of us cannot stand this sound), crunching, licking, swallowing, and talking with the mouth full. Other noises are drinking, burping, breathing heavily, tapping, and picking fingernails. There are many external noises—dogs barking, lawnmowers, music from cars, neighbours, headphones, mobile phones. The list is endless and one or many of these can cause problems to the point of having to wear earplugs. Unfortunately, there is no cure for this, but it can be managed with cognitive behavioural therapy and counselling. It is, however, important to address this issue as it can become obsessive and can create anger and frustration resulting in violent outbursts of temper.

Savant

Approximately half of savants have autism. The rest is down to central nervous system injury or disease. It is estimated that 10% of those with autism have some form of savant abilities. Savant is someone who seems to have learning difficulties but is, at the same time, exceptionally and highly gifted with one limited specialized field to the detriment of other abilities. For example; being a genius in mathematics or memory recall or being able to play a piece of music after hearing it only once. Others may be able to create a piece of artwork in great detail from memory. Unfortunately, for some they may be unable to complete simple everyday tasks for example cooking or personal hygiene. In some cases a carer may be needed as their inability to look after themselves may be quite severe.

Obsessive Compulsive Disorder

OCD is a type of anxiety disorder that manifests itself in repetitive behaviour and obsessions. Sufferers are often plagued with thoughts that are out of their control, such as feelings, impulses, and images. These can manifest as intrusive thoughts and can be based on worrying about everything and what may happen; if certain rituals are not followed, this may give rise to a fear of contamination and often brings about excessive hand washing and cleaning. Repetitive checking if doors are locked or switches are off, for example, which comes from a fear that something bad may happen if they don't do this a set number of times. Hoarding is another form of obsessional behaviour that, in extreme cases, will render sufferers unable to dispose of items in a rational way. There is a keen sense of order in some with OCD . This can easily be seen in the way items are carefully arranged in a cupboard or the order in which they dress which has to be adhered to every day. Having OCD does not always mean someone has autism.

Mysophobia

Mysophobia is also more commonly known as as germophobia, also known as baccillophobia and bacteriophobia as well as verminophobia and a common part of the OCD which is the pathological fear of contamination from germs. This is often seen in excessive hand washing. This can result in not using public lavatories for fear of germs and contamination. Sometimes this will result in people with mysophobia not entering public places, shaking hands, and using doorknobs without a glove or tissue covering their hands.

Depression

Depression affects around one third of us at some point in our lives so therefore the probability is many with autism will suffer depression at some point. However, for those people with autism it is considered they are at a higher risk. This could be down to communication problems and frustration. The other factor is that people with autism are less likely to go and seek help for their symptoms again because of lack of communication. This will often fester, and they will start to have behavioural problems such as repetitive or ritualistic behaviour and/or become more aggressive. OCD can be associated with autism and therefore could increase with anxiety and depression if it is not addressed. It is thought that around 50% of people with autism will suffer depression at some stage in their life, while the general statistic for this is rising to around 30% for those without autism. Signs to look out for are changes in behaviour. With depression, there could be signs of increased anxiety of symptoms they already have, as mentioned earlier, or a withdrawal of their usual self, maybe becoming withdrawn and quiet and in some cases the opposite of what they normally are. Extra vigilance in checking whether they are okay and happy is a good way to ensure that their well-being is maintained.

Epilepsy

Epilepsy and autism can be connected, and around a quarter of those with autism will have epilepsy. Scientists have found the genes that are linked to both. Epilepsy can cause people to have seizures and in autism it can be more difficult to spot as sometimes their behaviour can mimic the same signs as epilepsy. These seizures are caused by abnormal electrical activity in the brain. Mostly, those with epilepsy will have been diagnosed and treated with medication earlier in their childhood or teenage years. However, there can be an onset of epilepsy at any age. Epilepsy is controlled with medication.

Tourette Syndome

Tourette Syndrome is a neurological disorder which manifests itself with involuntary movements called 'tics'. This can affect any part of the body. Examples are eye blinking, twitching, throat clearing, sniffing, coughing, facial and movements. The other aspect to this is vocal. This can be a grunt, a repeated word or other sound. Rare cases have resulted in repetitive swear words. The University of California – San Francisco found that one in five children diagnosed with Tourette Syndrome meet the criteria for autism. There is no cure for this but there is treatment in the form of medications to help with this.

Dyspraxia

Dyspraxia is a condition that affects motor co-ordination. In the past this was referred to as 'Clumsy Child Syndrome.' This is because they can have trouble with spatial awareness, this can lead to them tripping, falling, bumping into things or even running or walking with an unusual gait. Tasks that involve catching, throwing may pose a problem as well as their dexterity being impaired which limits the use of scissors and in some severe cases the ability to hold a pencil or pen. Research has shown there is a more likelihood of someone with dyspraxia also having some form of autism, although it is possible to be diagnosed with Dyspraxia without the diagnosis of autism. Treatment varies between occupational therapy and cognitive behaviour therapy.

Communication and Language

Autism presents differently in each individual and is usually picked up within the first five years of childhood. A child may show signs through finding difficulties with social communication and interaction at school. This is the time when intervention should start. This may show itself as repetitive behaviour and meltdowns (this is usually down to an overload of the senses), which can manifest in screaming, crying, and even self-harming, rocking, lack of attention in lessons, and a bad reaction to sounds and light—all these are signs that may indicate autism.

 Autistic people have difficulties with interpreting both verbal and nonverbal language like gestures or tone of voice. Many have a very literal understanding of language and think people always mean exactly what they say. Understanding, tone of voice, jokes or sarcasm as well as body language and facial expressions may all prove to be a challenge for autistic people. The limited ability to communicate does not mean they do not understand anything. Although speech may be difficult for them, they may prefer to express themselves using sign language or visual symbols in some situations.

Some will have good language skills, but they may still find it hard to understand the expectations of others within conversations, sometimes repeating what they have just heard (this is called echolalia) or talking at length about their own interests. Autistic people often take things literally; therefore, they cannot understand some jokes.

 Autistic people often have difficulty reading the body language in others and often struggle knowing what is appropriate to say. To others this can come across as insensitive and distant. It is a struggle to empathize and understand the feelings and emotions in others. Although autistic people can be extremely sensitive to their own feelings, which can manifest itself in overreaction of their feelings, this can cause outbursts of anger or laughter that seems sometimes inappropriate. According to Wikipedia, "Globally, autism is estimated to affect 24.8 million people as of 2015. In the 2000s the number of people affected was estimated at one or two per 1,000 people worldwide. In the developed countries about 1.5% of children are diagnosed with autism spectrum disorder (ASD) as of 2017. The figure has approximately doubled from one in 150 from the year 2000 in the United States. It occurs four to five times more often in boys than girls. The number of people diagnosed has increased dramatically since the 1960s, partly due to changes in diagnostic practice; the question of whether actual rates have increased is unresolved."

Autistic people struggle with an unpredictable world that can become confusing and frightening to them. Daily routine is very important as they generally do not like change. Anything that disrupts their routine can cause anxiety and upset. As long as an individual is notified well in advance of change this can help to assuage the situation. Travelling the same way and eating the same foods are examples that can be beneficial in establishing a routine.

Highly Focused Interests

Highly focused interests can be very intense and obsessive with those with autism. This trait can be channelled in a very positive way. Many great inventors, and scientists, such as Albert Einstein, have been suspected of having had autism. Had it not been for these amazingly highly focused people then many discoveries we take for granted today may never have been invented. Repetitive work such as research or teaching may very well appeal to someone with Asperger's. Computer technology takes a great deal of highly focused attention too.

Sensitivity to Their Senses (Hypersensitivity)

Autistic people may experience an overload of sensitivity to noise, pain, temperatures touch, taste, smells, light, and colours which may distract them. Because they are too sensitive to everything that is going on around them, it is better for them to be in an environment that does not over stimulate their senses. This overstimulation can lead to distraction from whatever they are doing in a very negative way. When it comes to noises in the background, most of us can block some of these noises out, but someone with autism cannot, so background noises may overwhelm them, causing anxiety and pain. Touch can be a problem as sometimes they cannot cope with anyone crowding their space, which means no close contact at all. How they deal with this differs from individual to individual, but many will seek to escape this overload and leave the location that upsets them.

Lack of Sensitivity (Hyposensitive)

Hyposensitivity is the opposite to hypersensitivity, in which there is a lack of sensitivity. This condition may lead autistic people to seek stimulation of their senses which people are commonly aware of. Certain visual things such as something that sparkles can cause them to investigate and obsess over. Someone with this condition is more likely to be distracted by light, lots of colours, or sound and is drawn to it rather than being afraid of too much of it. Such people may become fascinated by something they see or hear. Unlike those too sensitive to touch, these people are more likely to want to touch. Hyposensitive people are more likely to want to feel their surroundings and be more tactile toward those around them. The normal feelings we have of temperature or pain is not felt by a number of people in this category. Noise may attract them and they may also create noise. This could result in tapping in order to stimulate their senses. This can cause them to leave a room or put their hands over their ears, and rock or scream. Any severe overload of these senses can lead to a meltdown. This, of course, can also lead them into self-harming.

Stimming

Stimming is considered to be a strategy for coping with anxiety that is often felt by those with autism. It can manifest itself in so many different ways like flapping, rocking, blinking excessively, pacing, head banging, biting, scratching, tapping, snapping fingers, and spinning objects or fiddling constantly with them. All of these will in some way give some form of release and is the only way they can deal with their anxieties. Stimming can be a clear indication that there is some underlying anxiety in their situation or surroundings that is making them feel uncomfortable. The other hypothesis is that stimming can release beta-endorphins which is pleasurable for those who rather than doing this as a result of negative feelings are doing the same for positive reasons. For some it is also about not having enough stimulation in their surroundings and they therefore feel it necessary to create their own.

Self-Harming

Self-harming is something that is a symptom also associated with people with autism. The cause is relatively unknown, but it is thought to be linked to depression or communication problems which can lead to frustration. Sometimes it is difficult to get across to people how they feel, what they are trying to say, or have problems with understanding. It could also be linked to an overload of their senses that they cannot cope with. Bullying, abuse, and being told off are also issues that they cannot handle and these again may come out in the form of self-harming. This is not the case with all those with autism or Asperger's though.

Violent outbursts against themselves can manifest in the following ways:-

Head banging—this is usually done by striking their head against walls or doors.

Hitting, biting, and scratching themselves— this may be with their own teeth, fingernails, or other sharp objects.

Cutting their selves with anything with a sharp edge (they have been known to carve their name on their skin in severe cases)

Pricking their skin with pins or needles

Pulling hair out

 Burning—this could be, for example, stubbing out a cigarette on their skin, using matches or an iron to do the same.

Abusing food and alcohol—this can be part of OCD whereby food and alcohol are taken to excess with little thought of the consequences to their health and if anyone becomes aware of these signs, then help is needed.

 It is important to find out why any of these things are happening, and with the right kind of approach, kindness, and a listening ear, the cause may be something that can be resolved. In a work placement, their communication skills should be good enough to relay their issues and problems. It could be something that is quite easily remedied like noise, by using headphones or earplugs. Too much light can be resolved by sunglasses. There are many solutions to their problems. Some, of course, may be a little more complicated, but it is important to get to the bottom of their problems before they become more serious.

Asperger's

Asperger's has been used as a diagnostic category from 1994 until 2013 when it was removed from the Diagnostic and Statistical Manual of Mental Disorders. The term Asperger's will continue to be used to describe this part of the Autistic Spectrum Disorder (ASD) as it is easier to separate the lesser degree of severity under the word 'Asperger's'. Asperger's is a term used to describe someone considered to be on the higher functioning side on the Autistic Spectrum Disorder and is not therefore a separate condition. While there are similarities between autism and Asperger's, people with Asperger's have a tendency to not be as severely affected as those described as autistic. People with Asperger's can have a higher intelligence and have better language and communication skills than those generally classed as autistic. The IQ of someone with Asperger's is more likely to be in the normal, high, or even superior range, but this is not often the case with someone with autism whose IQ is more likely to be in the lower range. Asperger's is a developmental disorder, mostly characterized by difficulties with nonverbal communication such as body language and some problems with social interaction. There are many differing degrees of the condition. It is impossible to cover every individual as each person is different. The reason why some people are born with this condition is as yet unknown, but there have been recent studies stating that the condition can run in families, and there are estimates that heritability can be as much as 83%, suggesting it may be genetic. It may seem that today there are many people with ASD; however, it could be that we are more aware of the condition due to more education and understanding. Today, children are being diagnosed very early in their lives, and recent studies are still on going.

Researchers in the field of autism have recently claimed to have identified subtle differences in the way affected babies respond to visual prompts. This has been done using eye-tracking technology on those babies that are considered to be more likely to have ASD, possibly due to having a sibling with this condition already. Monitoring the eye movements by checking the babies' ability to focus on various stimulations such as videos shown to them between two and 24 months of age may help determine if they are more likely to have ASD. It is unclear until later in the children's development as to where on the spectrum these children will be if at all. Today, we live in more enlightened times and early intervention can help in teaching coping strategies and how to fit into a future work environment. Many people with Asperger's will prove to be a great asset to many businesses as they often have outstanding capabilities that many employers would be very keen to have. There are many employed people today, who, with or without any diagnosis, are highly successful in their jobs. A diagnosis of Asperger's should not be seen as a negative development and should not stand in the way of one's employment if there is a better understanding of this condition from employers as well as colleagues. Many celebrities have come forward in recent years declaring they have Asperger's. Among these are Sir Anthony Hopkins, Anne Hegerty, Guy Martin, Daryl Hannah, Adam Young, Heather Kuzmich, Chris Packham, Susan Boyle and Tim Burton. Others considered to have Asperger's are Sir Alfred Hitchcock, Bill Gates, Michael Palin and Woody Allen to name but a few. From the past there are many who are believed to have been on the spectrum such as Charles Darwin, Hans Christian Anderson, Albert Einstein, Jane Austin, Sir Isaac Newton and George Orwell.

Myths and Misconceptions

Myths and misconceptions unfortunately play a big part in how people with autism are viewed, to the point that the saying that "a little learning is a dangerous thing" can sometimes be true. Films like "The Rain Man," although successful in creating more awareness about the condition, can also give a misconception that all those with ASD are like this and can do complicated maths in their heads but at the same time cannot look after themselves. While the character in this film was based on a real-life savant with superb recall, it is only one small example of autism. People can easily assume with this label that someone has an interest or a capability that they do not have. Assumptions should never be made that their interest is obsessional or they must be good with computers. While this may be the case in some circumstances, it is important to see each person as an individual and not indulge in assumptions. Upon seeing an announcement on social media that someone had been diagnosed with Asperger's it is sad to see that it was met with deep sympathy and pity in the same way as an illness which it is not. This is not helpful or positive. The correct way to approach this is to offer support alongside this diagnosis. While labels are a way of identifying a problem and allowing people to understand, they can also have a negative side to them which can lead to someone being treated differently, patronized, and being treated like they have learning difficulties when they do not; this can cause distress. If someone takes a little longer to understand something, for instance, it does not mean they do not understand anything at all. If their brain is, for example, taking in a problem, they may not only understand it, but may be trying to work out a solution without responding immediately. This can make them appear slow when they are just thinking. Autism is not one extreme and Asperger's is not the other, it is not as simple as that. One single trait does not put anyone in either category, but there are a number of interconnected traits that make them see the world differently from the way others perceive it.

Understanding and Acceptance

Understanding and acceptance is most important in order have a good working relationship and also to understand that this is a medically accepted condition that affects people's lives and interaction with others and not to make judgments because of it. Knowing the basics can prepare people to better understand the condition. In a work environment, instructions have to be clear and precise so there can be no misunderstanding. The literal understanding that many with Asperger's have is something one should remember as sometimes a generalization is not something that may be understood. For example, a timescale needs to be precise; just saying a couple of minutes will, in fact, mean two minutes to many with Asperger's. Being precise is important. Another example is "see you later." This to many with Asperger's is confusing. When? Where? Why? will be the questions that will immediately spring to their mind. Misunderstanding can lead to panic and stress, so it is best to be as factual as possible.

Asperger's in Industry

Routine will be very important to many with Asperger's. Working in a team may prove challenging to them and they may need plenty of support. While repetitive work will suit many of those with this form of autism, this cannot be assumed. There are those who will fit in very well in factory work for example. Some may be perfectionists and may voice their opinion if something is not done correctly. Unfortunately, while those with Asperger's may be very good at whatever they do, those around them will observe how others do the same job a little differently and pass judgment. This can be misunderstood as criticism when merely a fact is being pointed out. Therefore, instructions need to be clear at all times as general comments may be misunderstood. It may be the case with some employees with Asperger's that they may need prompting to have a break or when it is time to finish and go home. It is possible for them to get engrossed in what they are doing and lose track of time. This should never be taken advantage of. For many with Asperger's, completing a task will be very important and they may have difficulty stopping half way through something. This does make it a little difficult to stop for a break. This should be made very clear at the beginning. It should be noted that if it is a noisy environment, then it needs to be addressed to make sure they can cope with such an environment. If not, a solution can be found in the form of earplugs or headphones.

Asperger's in the Office

Those with Asperger's can in many cases work quite well in an office environment as long as they are very clear about what they are doing. In fact, they can be a great asset as their way of thinking is often abstract and problems can be resolved by this unorthodox approach. Also, often they will come up with innovative suggestions and ideas for improvement. Filing and sorting hold great appeal to such people with an organized brain. People with Asperger's may be very good at working with computers sometimes, but not always. Sometimes office work can suit them very well if they can work alone. This concept may be the best kind of work environment for many as they would be able to work best without any distractions.

Asperger's in Technology

Technology is an area where many with Asperger's will probably excel. Computers and technology are well suited to someone who would prefer to work alone and not want to interact with others. Problem-solving with computers is something that will fit very well with many with Asperger's. While we cannot assume that all those with Asperger's are good at computers, there have been some extreme cases where they have got into systems they should not have. This proves that some with Asperger's have extraordinary capabilities. Extraordinary recall would be an asset to any business, and the ability to fix a problem would be of great benefit. With such people, thinking is sometimes different and can, therefore, be much better than the average person.

Employment in General

There is no reason why people with Asperger's receiving adequate support would not make excellent employees as they are possibly more likely to be reliable, punctual, and have a professional and enthusiastic attitude to work. They can have a high level of attention to detail and are often better with routine and repetition, things that can be found in many jobs. However, strategies need to be put in place in order to get the best out of an employee with Asperger's syndrome. People with Asperger's may have difficulty in changing tasks. Multitasking may prove difficult to such people as sometimes they are better at doing one task at a time. Sometimes too many tasks to do or too many demands on them can cause a great amount of stress. They may have difficulty learning new tasks and transferring skills from one situation to another. Being left to make a decision may make them nervous. In some cases, people with Asperger's will need to be taught the things we would normally take for granted as being learnt from life experience and exposures. With Asperger's syndrome, there is a need for constant reinforcement and guidance to reduce the stress, confusion, and frustration that could possibly lead to understanding as well as behavioural difficulties. A withdrawal could mean that the person is feeling depressed and anxious because of stress and understanding difficulties. It is important that employers understand the difficulties of an employee with Asperger's as they need to provide a routine, structured environment with an element of predictability. Not all employees with Asperger's will excel in every job, but where they do find a job they fit in well, they are generally well respected, and with the right kind of support and understanding, they can make reliable and productive employees. In the workplace, people with Asperger's may require extra strategies to help them in their work, and these are as follows:

Strategies to Help in the Workplace

■■ Instructions need to be brief and precise and in some cases written down.

■■ Keep the language of instruction simple and uncomplicated.

■■ Confirm that the employee understands the task requested of him or her.

■■ Make sure work colleagues are aware of people with Asperger's and are able to help them when needed.

■■ Give the person time to take in the instructions.

■■ Provide a quiet place where people with this condition can work without distraction.

■■ Provide headphones and sunglasses in case they are required.

■■ Try to avoid jokes and sarcasm as these are often not understood by people with Asperger's.

Addressing Problems

■■ Look out for signs of sensory overload, such as rocking, covering ears/eyes, irritability, shutting down by not communicating and refusing to respond or interact, storming off quickly or showing any signs of aggression, anger or violence, and address the issue by talking before it becomes too stressful.

■■ Avoid meltdowns by intervening when people with Asperger's show signs of distress and take them to a secluded spot to discuss the issue that is causing them stress.

■■ If they are already having a meltdown, guide them to a quiet room and try to calm them down. Ask them if they wish to be left alone to sort themselves out. After they have calmed down, discuss the issue and try to resolve it so it is not repeated.

Author's Note

 Whilst working with children and one in particular who was diagnosed with Asperger's I became very interested in finding out as much knowledge as I could in order to cope with the challenges that such a child would bring. Partly excluded from school because of behaviour problems this child was to prove an interesting challenge in my care. Upon reading as much information as I could I soon realized how complex this condition was and how I had some of those traits myself. Many people like me will have certain traits of Autism but it really does depend on how much it impacts on your life as to whether it is worthwhile getting a diagnosis. For some a diagnosis is important especially if extra support and care is needed. Drawing from my own personal experience of Asperger's, it would be impossible to cover every aspect of this syndrome as there are so many variations to this condition. Some see it as a disability and others as an asset. It is not a subject that everyone will agree upon and even the experts in this field can change a diagnosis as was the case with the child I looked after being re-diagnosed with high IQ and low processing skills. Some people present with obvious signs of Asperger's that have somehow been missed and many will end up in mental health services. Although autism can share symptoms of those with mental health conditions, it is itself not a mental health condition. The right kind of help in mental health will depend very much on the awareness of autism itself. This in many cases can lead to a wrong diagnosis which is especially common in older people as they would not have had a diagnosis of this condition, particularly for those who were born before the 1970s. Toward the end of the twentieth century, much of the awareness of this condition was created; until then, very few people had even heard of it. People born in the earlier two thirds of the last century will often have had labels such as eccentric , different , odd and retarded. These were common descriptions of autism. Of course before then, around the turn of the twentieth century, many would have ended up in an asylum branded with all sorts of names such as cretin or simple, and even idiot. These were terms used too easily by people who had no understanding about the conditions people had that would make them stand out.

We have come a long way now and research is continuing to this day, and there is yet more to discover. It is important to keep a perspective on Asperger's as it is not an excuse for behavioural issues and problems but a reason, and hopefully with better understanding, a better work environment could be created for people with this condition. The types of jobs people with Asperger's can take up are incredibly varied. Teaching, research, and science provide the kind of repetitive work that suits people with this condition. Factory work, engineering, inventing, and creating are also suitable. In many situations, people with Asperger's can work very well alone. Many with Asperger's will be best suited to working on computers and technology. A problem-solving mind is also often associated with Asperger's. It is also now considered by some that Asperger's has been a valuable and positive development in our own evolution as very many inventors and gifted people, have retrospectively been considered to have Asperger's. They have given us many scientific breakthroughs that have provided solutions to many problems. I have personally never been diagnosed with Asperger's, but I am positive that I am on the spectrum. My father displayed many signs of Asperger's and my son too has many traits. While having differences, the traits we share are our determination, drive, and interests to the point of obsession. We all share the need to mend, fix and problem solve which does seem to be genetic. My grandfather too was a very difficult but inventive man and creative man. Routine and working alone have also been factors we all share. While some traits have been awkward to deal with, I do not see any of these as negative but, in fact, the opposite.

 As adults there is more awareness about ourselves, and we have all recognized ways in which to deal with our issues. As adults it is important to try and control our thoughts and handle them the best way we can. Many of the issues my son and I have had still exist, but they are being dealt with in a way that suits us. I have, as I mentioned before, met people with Asperger's; some cannot work, while others are proud to. One I remember at school used to pull his hair out regularly, this was out frustration of the condition that to this day has not been diagnosed. He has fitted well into a work environment, as routine is very important but on a social level was vulnerable to bullying due to his criticism of his work colleagues and the way things were done. He now works alone to which he is very well suited. In a work environment speaking one's mind without thought does not make for a good work environment. This is why it is so important to get a clearer understanding of the condition across to their work colleagues so there is a better and more harmonious work atmosphere. In certain circumstances allowances have to be made. A mere observational and factual comment can easily be misunderstood as blunt, rude and unpleasant when there was no malice intended at all.

Most of what I have written is based on what I have read from various experts added to my own knowledge and written in my own words. I have referred to Wikipedia and have read many articles by the National Health Service and other medical and scientific documents. Life experience and that of others with Asperger's have been a factor in my writing.

I have had published Jake Is Different— A Friendly Guide, a book about a young boy with autism, which has been beautifully Illustrated by Lynn Costelloe. This is a children's book that is suitable for parents, guardians, and teachers and is a useful tool that serves as an introduction to autism for children.

The Elf's Secret is another based on acceptance, self- esteem, confidence and self-awareness. Based on a boy elf who thinks he is different from the others, beautifully illustrated by Sarah Waterfield.

Website Resources

https://www.news-medical.net/health/Autism-History.aspx

https://www.nhs.uk/conditions/autism/

https://en.wikipedia.org/wiki/Savant_syndrome

https://en.wikipedia.org/wiki/Misophonia

https://en.wikipedia.org/wiki/Mysophobia

http://www.autism.org.uk/about/health/mental-health.aspx

http://www.navigocare.co.uk/wp-content/uploads/2016/08/Paper_2_what-is-autismleaflet-FINAL.pdf

https://en.wikipedia.org/wiki/Conditions_comorbid_to_autism_spectrum_disorders

https://www.epilepsy.com/learn/professionals/joint-content-partnership-aes/complex-relationship-between-autism-spectrum